MW01615995

Lifted

Devotional

You are
Loved?
 - Romans 5:8

by

Mary Teresa Fulp

Mary Teresa Fulp

ISBN: 978-0-578-53415-2

Dedication

This devotional is dedicated to my children, Damien, Patrick and Teresa. God loves you and so do I. Love you with all my heart...to the moon and beyond...all the way to the Heavens above! - Mom

I wrote this devotional during a challenging time in my life where I knew I needed to seek God with everything I had. He *Lifted* me to new heights as I stayed centered on His unconditional love.

It is my goal to honor Jesus with the way I live my life. I give Him all that I am with my lifted hands, heart and mind.

My goal with the *Lifted Reflections* journaling section in this devotional is to give the reader an opportunity to interact with the messages and make them their own. Ultimately, I hope the reader will begin to experience a deeper sense of love and belonging, knowing that God is with them every step of the way.

Contents

You have an amazing story

"All the days ordained for me were written in your book before one of them came to be." - Psalm 139:16

You have an amazing story that is ready to be written. How can you be sure? Because it was written by the Lord, God, Himself, before you were ever born. He chose you! He knew every twist of the plot and every unexpected turn, every joy and every sorrow. Wherever you go, He has already been. He will walk before you and with you. He promises to write your amazing story if you just give Him the pen.

Lord, show me how to live my life according to your perfect plan. You are the only author I want writing my amazing story. I choose to surrender the pen to Your mighty hand.

What do you hope is going to be written in the next part of your story?

God, I need you to write the rest of my story. I know my best days are ahead of me and I'm ready to give you the pen. Thank you for showing me that I need to put it in Your hands. Amen.

Lifted Reflections...

_____

_____

_____

_____

_____

_____

_____

_____

_____

_____

_____

_____

_____

_____

_____

_____

You are precious

"Out of all the people on the face of the earth the Lord has chosen you to be his treasured possession." - Deuteronomy 14:2

You are precious. You are His child worth searching for, worth saving, worth every sacrifice and when God counts up His heavenly treasures, He counts you! It is time for you to realize your true worth. You are a child of the King.

You have a purpose that makes you special and significant. Ignore your feelings and meditate on the truth of His word. Keep pressing, keep stepping, keep moving forward into your authentic gift. We need YOU!

Why did the Lord choose you? What makes you special and significant?

God, show me my purpose as I seek You with my whole heart. I want to honor You and live my live according to Your will. On the days I don't feel special, please give me the strength to see myself through Your eyes. Amen.

Lifted Reflections...

_____

_____

_____

_____

_____

_____

_____

_____

_____

_____

_____

_____

_____

_____

_____

_____

When it feels like everything is going wrong

"Come to Me, all you who are weary and burdened, and I will give you rest." - Matthew 11:28

When it feels like everything is going wrong, run to God. Take rest in Him. Remember, no matter what you do, no matter how bad things seem, He always loves you and is waiting for you to take refuge and rest in Him. If you don't know how to rest in Him, just say "Jesus I need you now. I need your peace to wash over me. I need your strength to face this day. I need your love to know that I am worthy." Be specific with your request and He will answer. He always answers when we seek him with our whole heart. He is a good, good Father!

Remember, no matter what you do, no matter how bad things seem, He always loves you and is waiting for you to take refuge and rest in Him.

What answers do you need from God so you can move forward?

God, thank you for beginning a good work in my life. Please show me the areas that are holding me back from living the abundant life you have for me. I need your guidance and direction as I move forward in Your name. Amen.

Lifted Reflections...

_____

_____

_____

_____

_____

_____

_____

_____

_____

_____

_____

_____

_____

_____

_____

_____

When we ask God to forgive us

"I, even I, am He who blots your transgressions, for my own sake, and remembers your sins no more." - Isaiah 43:25

When we ask God to forgive us, He does. This means when we make mistakes, we are free to move forward and try again to be the person He created us to be. He wants us to live in faith, love, peace and joy...every moment of every day. When doubt, fear and guilt appear, call out to Jesus and He will protect and carry us back to His loving, peaceful presence.

We block His blessings for our lives when we step away from His love. I want every blessing God has for my life and yours, that is why I do my best to remain obedient and in His presence of complete love and light each day. When we do this He works in and through us to bless everyone in our presence.

In what ways are you allowing God to work in your life?

God, I thank You for forgiving me and loving me the way You do. I want every blessing You have for my life. Thank You for showing me that when I am obedient I am able to live in Your love and light in ways that not only bless me, but bless those around me. In Jesus' Name, Amen.

Lifted Reflections...

_____

_____

_____

_____

_____

_____

_____

_____

_____

_____

_____

_____

_____

_____

_____

_____

_____

_____

Life can be very hard

"He gathers the lambs in His arms and carries them close to His heart." - Isaiah 40:11

Life can be very hard at times. The responsibilities and obligations can sometimes feel as if the weight of the world is resting on our shoulders, but this weight isn't ours to carry alone, it is His. When you are too tired to try again, you are too weak to keep going, or you've stumbled down one of life's steep slopes, throw your hands up to Him and say, "I can't do this on my own. I need you, God." The moment you reach up to Him, He reaches down to you, to lift you up and carry you close to His heart.

What are you carrying that is heavy? How can you give it to God?

Father, that thing that has a hold of me, I can make excuses for it. I can even reason it away. Today I put aside my excuses, and I choose Your best for me. Thank You for leading me towards what's beneficial and away from those fleshly things that potentially have power over my heart. In Jesus' Name, Amen.

Lifted Reflections...

_____

_____

_____

_____

_____

_____

_____

_____

_____

_____

_____

_____

_____

_____

_____

_____

_____

_____

When life knocks you down

"You are my hiding place, You will protect me from trouble and surround me with songs of deliverance." - Psalm 32:7

When life knocks you down, turn immediately to God and let Him heal your wounded heart. When you are filled with His strength you can go back and face life again. God loves it when we take refuge in Him and ask for His help. He loves to show us just how much He loves us. It's a love bigger and better than anything we can ever begin to imagine.

"No eye has seen, no ear has heard, and no mind has imagined the things that God has prepared for those who love him."
1 Corinthians 2:9

How can God help you today?

God, life has knocked me down more than once. I thank You for lifting me up and showing me that my brokenness has a purpose. Thank you for always being there for me even when I was too blind to see You. In Jesus' Name, Amen.

Lifted Reflections...

_____

_____

_____

_____

_____

_____

_____

_____

_____

_____

_____

_____

_____

_____

_____

_____

_____

He patiently knocks

"God is Love. Whoever lives in Love lives in God, and God in them." - 1 John 4:16

He patiently knocks until we answer and when we answer He moves in, because the place that God most loves to live is in us. Let Him in and become the truest, most beautiful YOU that you've ever been. His ways are so much higher than our own. Are you ready to be lifted? He is always ready to take us higher.

Where is God taking you? Are you ready to go where He needs you to go?

God, I'm so grateful that You continued to knock on the doors of my heart until I finally let You in. You are a patient and loving Father. Thank you for taking up residence in me. Please continue to lift and guide me to higher ground all the days of my life. Amen.

Lifted Reflections...

_____

_____

_____

_____

_____

_____

_____

_____

_____

_____

_____

_____

_____

_____

_____

_____

_____

_____

_____

Love

"Dear friends, let us love one another, for love comes from God. Everyone who loves has been born of God and knows God." - 1 John 4:7

Love. That's really what it's all about. More importantly, it's all about choosing love because love is a choice. This choice isn't always easy. To choose love we have to choose forgiveness and we have to respond to evil with kindness. When we do this, God sees our faithfulness and He returns an even bigger, deeper, more beautiful love to us.

How can you walk more in love this week?

God, show me the ways You want me to live and walk in your love this week. In Jesus' Name, Amen.

Lifted Reflections...

_____

_____

_____

_____

_____

_____

_____

_____

_____

_____

_____

_____

_____

_____

_____

_____

Be love

"Love is patient, love is kind. It does not envy, it does not boast, it is not proud. It does not dishonor others, it is not self-seeking, it is not easily angered, it keeps no record of wrongs. Love does not delight in evil but rejoices with the truth. It always protects, always trusts, always hopes, always perseveres." - 1 Corinthians 13:4-8

God loves to see His image in us. We are a reflection of His image when we choose to lift up the fallen, give to those in need, notice the unnoticed, forgive those who have wronged us, and walk daily with Him in complete faith, hope and love. He wants us to love others the way that He loves us.

In what ways is God wanting you to grow in love?

God, as I place my name in all the places love shows up in 1 Corinthians 13:4-8, please show me where my love is strong and where I am falling short. I want to grow in all the ways that You lead me in loving like You do. Amen.

Lifted Reflections...

_____

_____

_____

_____

_____

_____

_____

_____

_____

_____

_____

_____

_____

_____

_____

_____

_____

_____

You will shine

"You will shine among them like stars in the sky as you hold firmly to the word of life." - Philippians 2:15-16

You will shine when you know and live in truth. Choose to stand strong against the devil's schemes and continue to walk in faith with God. God loves it when we choose Him. He blesses us and protects us when we seek Him with all our heart. He will work everything out for the good of those who love, trust and believe in Him. His ways don't always feel good or make sense in the moment, but one thing I do know is He delivers on His promises and when He delivers, it is a much better outcome than anything we can humanly comprehend or do on our own.

Are you living your truth? How are you choosing to stand strong and walk in faith?

God, I want Your light and love to shine through me as I hold firmly to Your truth. Amen

Lifted Reflections...

_____

_____

_____

_____

_____

_____

_____

_____

_____

_____

_____

_____

_____

_____

_____

_____

_____

Every morning & evening

"Your word is a lamp to my feet and a light to my path." - Psalm 119:105

Every morning and evening I spend time in prayer. I ask God to show me what He needs me to do "today" to be the hands of Jesus. I ask that He direct my steps by speaking to my heart and giving me the courage to listen and act in complete obedience. My goal is to shine His love & light on others and leave them better as a result of my presence, which is ultimately His presence working in and through me.

"The one who says he abides in Him ought himself to walk in the same manner as He walked." - 1 John 2:6

In what ways is God calling you to be more like Jesus today?

God, thank you for directing my steps as I seek you to guide me each day. Thank you for giving me the courage to do what You need me to do to be a blessing in the lives of others. I ask that you continue to guide me to honor and glorify Your name. Amen.

Lifted Reflections...

_____

_____

_____

_____

_____

_____

_____

_____

_____

_____

_____

_____

_____

_____

_____

_____

_____

_____

If you want to love like Jesus

"Observe how Christ loved us. His love was not cautious but extravagant. He didn't love in order to get something from us but to give everything of himself to us. Love like that." - Ephesians 5:2

If you want to love like Jesus, you've got to love without limits.

Lord, I want to love like Jesus. I want to love with my whole heart. Help me give myself to others. Fill me with Your Spirit every moment of every day to love like You love. When people see me, let them see You. In Jesus' Name, Amen.

In what ways do you love like Jesus?

God, I want to love like you. I want to be consistent in this love walk. Search my heart and show me how to love without limits, especially during times I don't feel like it. Amen

Lifted Reflections...

_____

_____

_____

_____

_____

_____

_____

_____

_____

_____

_____

_____

_____

_____

_____

_____

_____

_____

Pray all day

"Pray continually." - 1 Thessalonians 5:17

Pray continually, constantly, unceasingly in all ways and at all times...over and over again. Pray in the shower, in the car, in the quiet of the morning, in the still of the night, in the midst of the busyness of the day...PRAY.

He will answer with incomprehensible peace, a love that lights up your heart, indescribable mercy and amazing grace. Oh yes, God loves it when we pray.

What does it look like in your life to pray continually? How can you improve your prayer life?

God, I don't always know how to pray, but I know that you understand my heart more than I do. I ask that You continue to strengthen my prayer life as I grow more intimately in my relationship with You. In Jesus' Name, Amen

Lifted Reflections...

_____

_____

_____

_____

_____

_____

_____

_____

_____

_____

_____

_____

_____

_____

_____

_____

_____

_____

No matter how you feel

Jesus turned and saw her. "Take heart, daughter," he said, "your faith has healed you." And the woman was healed at that moment. - Matthew 9:22

No matter how frightened, alone, untouchable and off the path you feel. You can be trembling, lost, confused and shattered...simply stretch out your hand in faith. Cry out to Jesus. Say, "Jesus I need You." There is power in His name. Jesus will hear your cry and feel you reach for Him. He will hear you. He will see you. He will welcome you with open arms. He treasures the touch of your faith. You can have faith the size of a mustard seed and He will grow it within you. When fear creeps in, put on the full armor of God. Immediately turn to Him and stand firm in your faith.

When was the last time you cried out to Jesus to receive healing?

God, there is great power in Your name. Sometimes I get overwhelmed with trying to figure it out on my own, especially when I don't see You working. I ask that you help me remain in trust and faith no matter how I feel. I want to rest on Your promises at all times. In Jesus' Name, Amen.

Lifted Reflections...

_____

_____

_____

_____

_____

_____

_____

_____

_____

_____

_____

_____

_____

_____

_____

_____

_____

_____

_____

God loves the way we fight

"Put on the full armor of God, so that you can take your stand against the devil's schemes." - Ephesians 6:11

Seriously...God loves the way we fight? Yes! There is a war going on in this world. A war for our hearts, minds, and souls. A war for our loved ones, and for strangers on the streets. It's a war to silence us, to make us invisible and miserable. It's a war to deny the power of God. It's time to put on the full armor of God and be prepared to fight. Fight for truth, faith, peace and love. Fight for the living Word of God. God loves the way we fight and take a stand for what is righteous.

What are you fighting for? Or what do you need to be fighting for?

God, I will continue to fight for Your truth. I will continue to be courageous and strong as I fight for all that You stand for. Thank you for convicting me to fight the good fight for You. Thank you for cutting away my flesh so that I know this fight is not about me. I know I must fight for what is righteous and good to glorify Your name. Amen.

Lifted Reflections...

_____

_____

_____

_____

_____

_____

_____

_____

_____

_____

_____

_____

_____

_____

_____

_____

_____

_____

You are on the right path

Your word is a lamp to my feet and a light for my path. - Psalm 119:105

You are on the right path when you seek God and listen more to Him and less to your doubts. He is leading you along the path He designed just for you. He goes before you, alongside you, and sometimes even carries you.

When you resist out of fear, He is such a loyal and loving Father that He will even drag you...kicking and screaming. You will get a little painfully torn up when you let fear take its grip. (Believe me...I know.)

One thing is for sure, you are never alone and it's a much more beautiful, peaceful and joyful journey when you choose to walk it with Him in disciplined faith and obedience. Do not expect others to fully understand His ways with you, just as you do not fully understand. Walk in obedience and do not let temptation or sin derail you. Stay on His path and when you are off, own it, repent and get back on.

He will reveal the staircase one step at a time. You will not see the complete staircase, therefore you must trust in Him with complete faith and take that next step as scary as it may seem, in obedience, knowing His ways are not your ways. He has big plans for your life and you will only get there if you lean not on your own understanding but on what He has placed on your heart.

Get out of your head and into your heart. Now cast your fears aside and take that next step in faith and follow Him. His way leads to your beautiful destination. His way delivers on the dream that only He knows about because He buried it deep within your heart. He is the Promiser and the Promise Keeper. Surrender. Let Him do His job. He loves to deliver on His promises.

How can you walk your path each day with less fear and more faith?

God, there is no fear in love. Thank you for giving me the strength to walk in the Spirit each day in blind faith. Help me remain obedient and at peace when I don't see the next step. I put my trust in You to be my chosen guide. Amen

Lifted Reflections...

_____

_____

_____

_____

_____

_____

_____

_____

_____

_____

_____

_____

_____

_____

_____

_____

It is so easy to let fear in

"Have I not commanded you? Be strong and courageous. Do not be afraid; do not be discouraged, for the Lord your God will be with you wherever you go." - Joshua 1:9

It is so easy to let fear creep in when we are about to take a leap of faith, or when we take a bold stand for what is righteous. When that happens, immediately turn to God. Say, "Jesus, I need You. I can do all things with and through You. I trust You and I am strong because of You!"

Now go big and be bold for you are created in His image and He doesn't play small. Remain humble in the process, knowing all you do is to honor and glorify Him. Use your spiritual gift to lead people to His amazing grace, light and love!

Where has fear crept into your life and kept you small?

God, I desire to live bold in who you created me to be. I do not want to please people. I want to please You with the way I live my life. In Jesus' Name, Amen.

Lifted Reflections...

_____

_____

_____

_____

_____

_____

_____

_____

_____

_____

_____

_____

_____

_____

_____

_____

_____

_____

His grace is enough

But he said to me, "My grace is sufficient for you, for my power is made perfect in weakness." Therefore I will boast all the more gladly about my weaknesses, so that Christ's power may rest on me. That is why, for Christ's sake, I delight in weaknesses, in insults, in hardships, in persecutions, in difficulties. For when I am weak, then I am strong. - 2 Corinthians 12:9-10

His grace is all we need. His power works best in our weakness. When we depend on Him continually our entire perspective changes. I have known the struggle of depending on myself, up until the last few years. I'm so grateful that I know now how amazing it is when He works on my behalf. I seek Him, pray and then give my prayer requests to Him to work out in His time. I then get to thoroughly enjoy life. He wants to take care of us. We just need to let Him. You will begin to see miracles happening all around you the moment you truly believe and trust in God with all your heart. He is such a good, good Father!

What was the last thing you gave to God or asked Him to help you with?

God, I know your power works best in weakness. When I'm feeling weak, help me remember to turn to You instead of going back to old habits. I want to get to a place in my life where my natural instinct is to immediately turn to You when I am weak, knowing that in my weakness You are strong. Amen.

Lifted Reflections...

_____

_____

_____

_____

_____

_____

_____

_____

_____

_____

_____

_____

_____

_____

_____

_____

_____

God loves you

"I praise you because I am fearfully and wonderfully made; your works are wonderful, I know that full well." - Psalm 139:14

God loves you, because you are YOU! He loves your imperfections, your silliness, your creativity, your authenticity and your unique spiritual gift. He loves that you are courageous, confident, joyful and kind. He loves the way you laugh, the way you cry, the way you work and the way you give. He loves that you trust Him enough to call on Him and seek Him. God loves that you are fearfully and wonderfully made in His image. You are a child of God. Enjoy it. Be blessed and live loved.

What does God love about you? What is it that sets you apart from everyone else?

God, thank you for loving me unconditionally. I love the way you love all of me. Help me to see myself through Your eyes so that I too, can love my imperfect self the way you love me. Amen.

Lifted Reflections...

_____

_____

_____

_____

_____

_____

_____

_____

_____

_____

_____

_____

_____

_____

_____

Do all things in love

"So that Christ may dwell in your hearts through faith. And I pray that you, being rooted and established in love, may have power, together with all the Lord's holy people, to grasp how wide and long and high and deep is the love of Christ, and to know this love that surpasses knowledge—that you may be filled to the measure of all the fullness of God." - Ephesians 3:17-19

We must be open to receiving love from God. The more we rest in Him, the more freely His blessings flow in and through us. It is in the light of His love that we are transformed into His image. By spending time with Him in the Word (reading scripture, the Bible) we begin to absorb how long, wide and deep His love truly is for us. Sometimes what He offers us seems too good to be true. Do not second guess it or turn from Him. His love is amazing and will feel too good to be true when we compare it to what we have known love to be in this world. He will keep pouring his abundant love into us if we remain open to receiving and faithful to Him. There is a direct correlation to receiving and believing. We must believe in order to receive the fullness of His love. As we trust Him more and more, we will receive more and more from Him. The more we receive, the more we are able to give. We are His image-bearers. He wants the world to see and receive His magnificent love through us.

Are you open to receiving love from God?

God, I say that I'm open to receiving Your love and then I see something about myself that shows me I haven't completely opened my heart to receiving all that You have for me. Thank you for revealing these things about myself that are holding me back. I will continue to seek You with all my heart and enjoy the process as you lift me higher. Amen.

Lifted Reflections...

_____

_____

_____

_____

_____

_____

_____

_____

_____

_____

_____

_____

_____

_____

_____

_____

_____

God knows we don't understand His ways

"The Lord rewards everyone for their righteousness and faithfulness." - 1 Samuel 26:23

God knows there are times when we don't understand His ways and He sees us continue to follow Him even when His choices make us feel angry, frustrated or sad. He sees us continue to choose to fix our eyes on Him in the midst of our pain and sorrow. He knows the times we feel too exhausted to carry on. He loves it when we lean into Him and let Him carry us. Faithfulness when we are confused, hurt and exhausted is what He sees, what He loves and what He rewards. Your blessing is coming. Stay the course!

How do you stay the course when you don't understand His ways?

God, I trust You even when I don't understand where You are taking me. I will work hard to remain consistent in my daily habits to spend time with You so that I can remain centered in Your love and keep You in Your proper place in my life. I will walk by faith and not by feelings or fear. In Jesus' Name, Amen.

Lifted Reflections...

_____

_____

_____

_____

_____

_____

_____

_____

_____

_____

_____

_____

_____

_____

_____

_____

_____

_____

Show up where love is needed

"So now I am giving you a new commandment: Love each other. Just as I have loved you, you should love each other. Your love for one another will prove to the world that you are my disciples." - John 13:34-35

Jesus wants us to include His love in our interactions with others. He wants us to show up where love is needed. He wants us to reflect His image in the way we treat others. He wants us to do this all the time and to all people, not some of the time and to some people. I will start with myself and the people nearest me. I will do small things with GREAT love each day.

Where is God directing you to show up where love is needed?

Dear God, Your love for people is beautiful. You love everyone. You love when there's nothing to gain in return. You love me when I fall short. Help me to show up, as You lead me to where love is needed. In Jesus' Name, Amen.

Lifted Reflections...

_____

_____

_____

_____

_____

_____

_____

_____

_____

_____

_____

_____

_____

_____

_____

_____

We all struggle

"'If you can'?" said Jesus. "Everything is possible for one who believes." Immediately the boy's father exclaimed, "I do believe; help me overcome my unbelief!" - Mark 9:23-24

We all struggle with this at certain times in our lives. We need to develop discipline to turn to the Word and to Jesus through prayer (and fasting) regardless of how we feel. We need to walk through the darkness to get to the light. It will feel uncertain and frightening at times. Keep seeking God and He will direct our paths. He will calm the storm. He will carry us through the darkness into His glorious light. We just need to be open to hearing, seeing and receiving His love. Resist the temptation to shut down or turn away from His love when life is hard. Always choose faith over fear. Love over hurt. Joy over sadness. Hope over despair. Him over the enemy. What we choose will grow within our hearts and minds. Choose wisely. Choose LOVE.

What are you choosing to let grow in your heart and mind?

God, help me overcome my unbelief. I know that the struggles I face are preparing me for what You have called me to do. You are creating an excellent work in me. May I consider it pure joy, knowing that the outcome of this struggle is for Your highest good. Amen.

Lifted Reflections...

_____

_____

_____

_____

_____

_____

_____

_____

_____

_____

_____

_____

_____

_____

_____

_____

_____

Heart work

"But blessed are your eyes, for they see: and your ears, for they hear." - Matthew 13:16

What do you see and hear with your heart? When we open our eyes and ears with our heart to God, we will see and hear Him. He always does His work deep inside of us at the heart level. When you look and listen for God, you'll discover He's everywhere. He loves it when we open our eyes to see Him and our ears to hear Him. He loves it when we invite Him in so He can live in our hearts and direct our path to experience his loving presence with each step we take. Live loved and walk with Him in complete joy and peace!

How do you take time to see and hear from God throughout the day?

God, thank you for guiding me. Help me to see and hear from you with clarity in the midst of the noise that sometimes causes me to be distracted and lose my focus. If I get lost, may it be in doing the heart work that pleases You. In Jesus' Name, Amen.

Lifted Reflections...

_____

_____

_____

_____

_____

_____

_____

_____

_____

_____

_____

_____

_____

_____

_____

_____

_____

Kind thoughts should be spoken

"Kind words are like honey— sweet to the soul and healthy for the body." - Proverbs 16:24

When you think kind thoughts about something or someone, have the courage to speak them. We never know the power of our words, because they have a ripple effect with no logical end. Speak genuine words of life & love into those you come into contact with. You may just be the one person who offers a gift at the time that has the power to keep someone going or even turn a life around. Always speak the positive truth and be present enough to notice others. Kindness matters more than we know. Take the time to lift someone up today with genuinely kind words spoken from the heart.

Do you think and speak kind thoughts? How can you grow in this area?

God, show me how and where I need to grow in noticing good things about others. Give me the courage to take the time to speak life into others with the truth that You place on my heart and mind. In Jesus' Name. I pray, Amen.

Lifted Reflections...

_____

_____

_____

_____

_____

_____

_____

_____

_____

_____

_____

_____

_____

_____

_____

_____

_____

The beauty of surrender

"Now to him who is able to do immeasurably more than all we ask or imagine, according to his power that is at work within us." - Ephesians 3:20

What a beautiful difference it makes in our lives when we surrender and let Him work in and through us. Lord show me what you need me to do today and give me the courage and discipline to do it. Thank you for what You have already done and are currently doing. There is nothing like Your love and grace. I ask that you give me the patience to trust in Your plan and Your will as I continue to submit and walk in complete obedience with You. Today is a gift and I will seek You in every moment of it.

What is the Lord revealing to you that He needs you to surrender to Him so He can go to work in your life?

God, I tend to want to be in control. Please show me what you need me to give to You so that I can do my part and put my trust in You to do Yours. Amen.

Lifted Reflections...

_____

_____

_____

_____

_____

_____

_____

_____

_____

_____

_____

_____

_____

_____

_____

_____

_____

When we feel inadequate

"He heals the brokenhearted and binds up their wounds." - Psalm 147:3

When we are feeling inadequate, worried or scared about anything in life, know that God is always working on our behalf. We don't always understand why, but we know God does. Lean into the truth this psalm continues to share: "The LORD delights in those who fear him, who put their hope in his unfailing love" - Psalm 147:11

Sometimes the best thing we can do is rest and wait. Other times He is calling us to action. Seek Him and continue to put your best foot forward, one step, one decision at a time. He will make a masterpiece of our mess. He will use our brokenness to heal others. He will bind up our wounds and show us the purpose for them…in time.

I'm grateful for the painful twists and turns in life that have brought me closer to Him. I am blessed and beginning to see myself the way He sees me. I am a beautiful child of God.

What do you do when you feel inadequate?

God, when I am feeling inadequate it's easy for me to begin to doubt my worth. Thank you for showing me that I'm worthy for who I am in You, especially on days when I'm feeling less than good enough. Thank you for being quick to remind me that I find my worth in You. In Jesus' Name, Amen.

Lifted Reflections...

_____

_____

_____

_____

_____

_____

_____

_____

_____

_____

_____

_____

_____

_____

_____

_____

_____

Peace

"Peace I leave with you; my peace I give you. I do not give to you as the world gives. Do not let your hearts be troubled and do not be afraid." - John 14:27

Peace. What an awesome gift He gives us. All we have to do to experience more peace is get rid of distractions and take time to sit quietly in His presence. Seek Him and know that He will fill us with the gift of peace.

My daughter and I met my mom at church last night. Side by side, we sat in the presence of God. Three generations of beautiful God-fearing women were listening to the Word together and experiencing peace like none other.

Cast out all fear, worry and doubt and meditate on the Word to enjoy the fullness of the peace that only He can give. It is such a breathtakingly beautiful experience to feel His peace wash over you.

How are you making time to seek and receive His peace?

God, your peace continues to amaze me. You provide such a perfect peace in the midst of some crazy storms. I will continue to seek Your peace and rest in Your presence so that I may be a beacon of Your light in the darkness. Amen.

Lifted Reflections...

_____

_____

_____

_____

_____

_____

_____

_____

_____

_____

_____

_____

_____

_____

_____

_____

_____

Be Strong & Courageous

"Have I not commanded you? Be strong and courageous! Do not tremble or be dismayed, for the LORD your God is with you wherever you go." - Joshua 1:9

What an amazing difference it makes when we lean on this understanding. Be strong and courageous for He is with us wherever we go. This is a game changer in the game of life. God calls us to do more with the gift he has given us.

Are you going to live strong and courageous in order to make the dash between the moment you arrived and departed count? I hope so! We need you to live the life you were born to live. Rise strong from setbacks. We need to know the real you while there is still time. After all, we are all just walking each other home. Let's make it an amazing walk by living our purpose and passion with complete authenticity. We were born to shine!

How can you choose to be strong and courageous even when you aren't feeling strong?

God, I know I am strong in and through You. Thank you for being with me wherever I go. I will continue to seek Your face so I can be strong and courageous even on days where I am feeling weak. I want to honor and glorify You with the way I live my life. In Jesus' Name, Amen.

Lifted Reflections...

_____

_____

_____

_____

_____

_____

_____

_____

_____

_____

_____

_____

_____

_____

_____

_____

Put on Love

"Love bears all things, believes all things, hopes all things, endures all things." - 1 Corinthians 13:7

Put on and receive His love in order to love more and live fearless.

Seek God with your whole heart. He will show you an unwavering love that will begin to take root inside of you as you interact with people. It is such an incredible blessing to love ourselves and others the way that He loves us.

How is His love taking root inside of you?

God, may I continue to seek you with my whole heart so that I can put on Your love before I leave the house each day. May my actions be motivated by Your heart. In Jesus' Name, I pray. Amen.

Lifted Reflections...

_____

_____

_____

_____

_____

_____

_____

_____

_____

_____

_____

_____

_____

_____

_____

_____

_____

Serve others in Love

"You, my brothers and sisters, were called to be free. But do not use your freedom to indulge the flesh; rather, serve one another humbly in love." - Galatians 5:13

This verse is completely on my heart today, to the point I'm in tears as I thank God for calling me to humbly serve others in love. The more I spend time with Him, the more He directs my path to serve as an instrument of His peace and love. I'm grateful for my life's journey that brought me to where I am today...with eyes to see, ears to hear and a heart that is totally fixed on Him.

"Amazing grace! how sweet the sound,
  That saved a wretch; like me!
I once was lost, but now am found,
  Was blind, but now I see."

I grew up singing that song in church. I have always loved it and now that I understand the deeper meaning, I love it even more. Thank you, Jesus!

How can I serve others in love today?

God, I ask that as you free me from living according to the ways of the world, that you use me as a vessel to free others as well. You have called me by name and have set me apart. May I remember this as I go about my daily tasks, so that I may serve others humbly in love. Amen.

Lifted Reflections...

_____

_____

_____

_____

_____

_____

_____

_____

_____

_____

_____

_____

_____

_____

_____

_____

_____

Eyes fixed on Him

"Those who look to him are radiant; their faces are never covered with shame." - Psalm 34:5

I have found that keeping my eyes fixed on Him is the best way to live.

You are radiant. You are a gift. Thank you for letting His radiant light shine through you to bless the lives of all who experience your loving presence!

Are you keeping your eyes fixed on Him? How do you adjust your focus when you get caught up in the busyness of life?

God, I seek you each day and ask that you strengthen my focus so that no amount of noise or distraction from the enemy can cause me to stumble and lose my focus. May I always keep you in your proper place, for You are my rock and redeemer. Amen.

Lifted Reflections...

_____

_____

_____

_____

_____

_____

_____

_____

_____

_____

_____

_____

_____

_____

_____

_____

_____

He works everything out

"And we know that God causes everything to work together for the good of those who love God and are called according to his purpose for them." - Romans 8:28

Before I believed and trusted in God with all my heart, I was so confused as I tried to understand the unplanned chaos that happens throughout life when things don't go according to plan or when something happens that is completely unexpected that causes you to change course completely. I would always go into "fix-it" mode and begin to create a new plan to adjust to the circumstances.

I am so incredibly grateful that God, through my brokenness and inability to fix everything, showed me that when I trust and believe in Him with all my heart and walk in obedience and complete faith, He orchestrates the most beautiful outcomes, better than anything I can possibly imagine on my own.

Today, I am thankful to know that he is working everything out for the good of those who love Him and seek him wholeheartedly.

What am I believing and trusting God to do in my life?

God, I don't always understand what you are doing, but I do know that you are working everything out for the good of those who love You. I love You and trust what You are doing in my life. Thank you for being YOU. Amen.

Lifted Reflections...

An amazing and delicious life

"Whatever you do, work at it with all your heart, as working for the Lord, not for human masters, since you know that you will receive an inheritance from the Lord as a reward. It is the Lord Christ you are serving." - Colossians 3:23-24

When we seek to please others we begin to lose the very thing that makes us special. In fact, we actually please more people when we are most true to our authentic self. When we live according to the person God created us to be, in His image, we are powerful beyond measure.

By seeking and submitting to God, I have been able to walk in peace as I live my purpose with passion and joy. I am learning how to protect my time and maximize my energy for what He has called me to do. I have had to say no to some good things that weren't in line with my highest purpose, in order to say yes to the things that are.

Now that I am more clear about who I am, I am doing things daily that are aligned with my true purpose and, in turn, my life is turning out to be AMAZALICIOUS!

Do you want an AMAZALICIOUS life? What does that even mean? A life that is both amazing and delicious. What adjustments can you make to manifest the dreams that God buried deep in your heart?

God, I will do my part to seek and submit to Your will for my life. I know what you have created me to do is going to give me the AMAZALICIOUS life I deeply desire. Your best is what I'm holding out for. In Jesus' Name, Amen.

Lifted Reflections...

_____

_____

_____

_____

_____

_____

_____

_____

_____

_____

_____

_____

_____

_____

_____

_____

_____

_____

Perfect peace

"You will keep in perfect peace those whose minds are steadfast, because they trust in you." - Isaiah 26:3

Perfect peace. Praise God. I'm so grateful for the spiritual leaders in my life who teach me how to spend my time meditating on the Word to attain this beautiful blessing from God. He provides us perfect peace when we are steadfast in our walk with Him.

Spend time meditating on the Word each day. Carve out time day and night and you will receive perfect peace, along with many other countless blessings. Thank you, Jesus, for pouring Your perfect peace and love into my heart, mind and spirit. I'm eternally grateful and will honor You in my daily walk with others.

How do you or can you carve out time each day to meditate on the Word in order to grow stronger in Christ?

God, You give us a peace that surpasses all understanding. I pray that those who are reading this will experience a new level of what it means to be lifted by Your perfect peace. In Jesus' Name, Amen.

Lifted Reflections...

_____

_____

_____

_____

_____

_____

_____

_____

_____

_____

_____

_____

_____

_____

_____

_____

Today marks the day

"See, I am doing a new thing! Now it springs up; do you not perceive it? I am making a way in the wilderness and streams in the wasteland." - Isaiah 43:19

Today marks the day that I received the answer from God about how He wants me to proceed with the work He has called me to do. I have been searching for answers for a few years now and have been praying about next steps. He is the great revealer. He is the Promise Keeper. When He places something on our heart, all we need to do is remain in obedience through complete trust and pure faith. He will provide the answers in His time. I spend time alone with Him daily. I used to try to figure it all out on my own. Now that I know better, I do better.

Wow, I am so grateful that I am learning to listen and be patient for His answers and direction. He knows my heart and He directs my path.

Thank you, Jesus, for loving me so deeply and lighting my path in such a magnificent way.

When was the last time you received an answer from God? What question do you have for Him today?

God, thank you for loving me so deeply and lighting my path in such a magnificent way, so that I too can be a light for others who need You. Amen.

Lifted Reflections...

_____

_____

_____

_____

_____

_____

_____

_____

_____

_____

_____

_____

_____

_____

_____

_____

_____

_____

_____

_____

When we know better

"In the morning, Lord, you hear my voice; in the morning I lay my requests before you and wait expectantly." - Psalm 5:3

When we know better, we do better. I now wake up at least 30 minutes earlier than I used to so that I can spend time in prayer. Reading scripture and meditating on the Word of God has brought forth so much clarity in my life. "What a beautiful name it is, the name of Jesus Christ our King!"

Thank you, Jesus, for hearing my requests and delivering on them in unimaginable ways. Today I reflect on how grateful I am to be known and loved by You.

What are you doing better now that you know better?

God, thank you for hearing my requests and delivering on them in unimaginable ways. Today I reflect on how grateful I am to be known and loved by You. In Jesus' Name, Amen.

Lifted Reflections...

_____

_____

_____

_____

_____

_____

_____

_____

_____

_____

_____

_____

_____

_____

_____

_____

_____

_____

_____

Understanding on a deeper level

"For the word of God is living and active *and* full of power [making it operative, energizing, and effective]. It is sharper than any two-edged sword, penetrating as far as the division of the soul and spirit [the completeness of a person], and of both joints and marrow [the deepest parts of our nature], exposing *and* judging the very thoughts and intentions of the heart." – Hebrews 4:12

I am understanding on a deeper level why I was so hesitant for so many years to open the Bible. I always thought it was because it was overwhelming to read...that I didn't know how or where to get started. I was confused by the depth of it and wanted to truly understand, so I chose to let it sit and collect dust.

I am grateful to have reached a new level of understanding that will only grow stronger in time. I now realize I had to be ready to do the gut wrenching heart work that is exposed by the active and alive words in the Bible. It has been a painfully beautiful process of becoming, the woman He created me to be, as I ask God to search my heart and give me the strength to work through and release the sin that is exposed in the process of making my heart pure again.

I am now committed to keeping my heart pure and beautiful by turning to the Word and growing the seeds of LOVE.

What new level of understanding have you reached today?

God, I desire to grow in my relationship with you throughout life. I ask that You continue to take me to a deeper level of understanding what You need me to do to live my life to honor You. In Jesus' Name, Amen.

Lifted Reflections...

_____

_____

_____

_____

_____

_____

_____

_____

_____

_____

_____

_____

_____

_____

_____

_____

_____

_____

He is a patient & loving Father

"Here I am! I stand at the door and knock. If anyone hears my voice and opens the door, I will come in and eat with that person, and they with me." - Revelation 3:20

He is such a patient and loving Father. He waits at the door until we invite Him in. He waited for decades until I finally got to a point, through my brokenness, that I said, "Jesus, I need you. I can't do this on my own." That's all it took. Just like that. He came in and began to make my heart His home.

Are you making Him wait outside or have you opened the door to your heart and invited Him in?

God, my heart is Your home. I invite You to do any cleaning You deem necessary for my growth. I know I like to hold onto things that aren't necessary. I ask that You pack up and remove anything that doesn't serve Your purpose. As much as it may hurt, I know You are doing it for my good and I trust Your plan for my life. In Jesus' Name, Amen.

Lifted Reflections...

_____

_____

_____

_____

_____

_____

_____

_____

_____

_____

_____

_____

_____

_____

_____

_____

_____

Seeking peace

"You will keep in perfect peace those whose minds are steadfast, because they trust in you." - Isaiah 26:3

I was seeking peace for so long, and didn't receive it until I fixed my eyes completely on Christ. All else fell into place so peacefully when I placed Him as my #1. I never realized how beautiful the love and peace that only He can give really is.

He gives a perfect peace to us, when we get to a place where we know it will all go according to His perfect plan. This happens when we are faithful and obedient, keeping our eyes, mind and heart fixed on Him.

How do you seek His peace daily?

God, as I seek Your perfect peace in my life on a daily basis, I thank You for providing it no matter how I feel or no matter what I'm facing. Thank you for showing others that they too can seek Your peace and glow from within during times that they may otherwise feel like throwing in the towel. Amen.

Lifted Reflections...

_____

_____

_____

_____

_____

_____

_____

_____

_____

_____

_____

_____

_____

_____

_____

_____

_____

All heart

"Whatever you do, work at it with all your heart, as working for the Lord, not for human masters." - Colossians 3:23

When we work at it with all our heart, we make a deeper, more meaningful impact. Have you noticed that some people appear to be on fire for their life's purpose? While others appear to be going through the motions? What is the difference? When we know our why and live in our authentic purpose, the passion for our calling lights our way. I choose to work at it with all my heart, and in doing so, hope to inspire others to do the same.

Do you know your why? What are you working at with all your heart?

God, as I seek Your will for my life, my why becomes more clear. I choose to work at what You have called me to do with all my heart. Thank you for calling me out of the darkness and into Your radiant light. In Jesus' Name, Amen.

Lifted Reflections...

_____

_____

_____

_____

_____

_____

_____

_____

_____

_____

_____

_____

_____

_____

_____

_____

_____

_____

Uplifting people

"My heart is inditing a good matter: I speak of the things which I have made touching the king: my tongue is the pen of a ready writer." - Psalm 45:1

I love it when I'm around uplifting people who know the Word and drop the seeds of wisdom onto my fertile soil. I was just thinking and speaking about how powerful the heart truly is.

I've learned some valuable lessons throughout life when I made choices that were not in line with the Word of God. I'm still in the process of learning how critical it is to only sow the good seeds of His love. I'm in the beginning stages of understanding through His wisdom and truth, how to guard, protect and nurture my own heart.

The process of cleansing the heart of the bad seeds that have taken root is a painful and necessary process in order to have it be a heart where the goodness and abundance of God's love can live, multiply and flow.

I have asked Him over and over again, to search my heart and help me release the parts that are not pure. I'm so grateful for His love and forgiveness as I return to the person who He created in His image from the moment the seeds of love were planted and sown.

How's your heart? Are you doing the necessary work to cleanse and purify it?

God, thank you for beginning a good work in me and finishing it as I grow stronger each day in You. In Jesus' Name, Amen.

Lifted Reflections...

_____

_____

_____

_____

_____

_____

_____

_____

_____

_____

_____

_____

_____

_____

_____

_____

_____

_____

Love more & judge less

"Do not judge, or you too will be judged. For in the same way you judge others, you will be judged, and with the measure you use, it will be measured to you." - Matthew 7:1-2

The more judgmental the person, the more unhappy they are. When we judge others we are learning about deeper unresolved matters within ourselves.

When we begin to love more and judge less, we reach a new level of freedom to become our most authentic, beautiful, amazing self. When this happens the people who also radiate love and kindness will naturally gravitate into our lives, while those who don't will naturally gravitate away.

Lesson: Be love. Don't you dare dim your light for the comfort of others.

I love how God works everything together for the good of those that love and honor Him.

What is one area you can judge less and love more?

God, I ask that You correct me each time I pass judgment. I ask that You show me how to love more and judge less in ways that honor and glorify You. In Jesus' Name, Amen.

Lifted Reflections...

_____

_____

_____

_____

_____

_____

_____

_____

_____

_____

_____

_____

_____

_____

_____

_____

_____

Renewed Strength

"But those who hope in the Lord will renew their strength. They will soar on wings like eagles; they will run and not grow weary, they will walk and not be faint." - Isaiah 40:31

I have experienced this renewed strength firsthand and have been fortunate to witness it over and over again in the lives of others. I'm so grateful for my own journey that has led me to this new understanding. It is a beautiful process to see the transformational power of the Holy Spirit working in and through those who put their unwavering hope in the Lord.

How does putting your hope in the Lord help you? Where do you need renewed strength in your life?

God, the renewed strength You offer me each morning keeps me going strong. I thank You for giving me the strength I need to face each day victoriously. Amen.

Lifted Reflections...

_____

_____

_____

_____

_____

_____

_____

_____

_____

_____

_____

_____

_____

_____

_____

_____

_____

What we sow grows

"Be not deceived; God is not mocked: for whatsoever a man soweth, that shall he also reap. For he that soweth to his flesh shall of the flesh reap corruption; but he that soweth to the Spirit shall of the Spirit reap life everlasting. And let us not be weary in well doing: for in due season we shall reap, if we faint not." - Galatians 6:7-9

Whatever a person sows, that and only that, is what grows. What are you sowing? Seeds of love or seeds of hate? Seeds of truth or seeds of lies? Seeds of kindness or seeds of hurt? Seeds of faith or seeds of fear? Seeds of trust or seeds of distrust? Keep in mind that what we sow grows stronger in our lives and the lives of those around us.

I choose to sow seeds of kindness, respect, truth, humility, gratitude, positivity, faith, hope and, above all these, love.

What are you sowing? What do you need to sow more of?

God, I know the seeds I sow will grow and reap a harvest, therefore I will intentionally choose to sow seeds of love motivated by a pure heart and will reap a mighty harvest of Your love in return. Amen.

Lifted Reflections...

_____

_____

_____

_____

_____

_____

_____

_____

_____

_____

_____

_____

_____

_____

_____

Wait on the Lord

"Wait on the Lord: be of good courage, and he shall strengthen thine heart: wait, I say, on the Lord." - Psalm 27:14

"And let us not be weary in well doing: for in due season we shall reap, if we faint not." - Galatians 6:9

Wait on the Lord and keep doing good regardless of how you feel. Wait and do good. Wait and do good. When we grow tired and weary, the Lord renews our strength. It is important to keep on keeping on...doing what we know is right, for in due season we will reap, if we stay the course and continue to do the good He has called on us to do.

Today I turn in faith to God to strengthen and renew my heart, for He knows me intimately, loves me completely and is in control of my future.

How are you waiting on the Lord? What are you waiting expectantly for?

God, help me to dream dreams that are too big for me to accomplish on my own. I want to have Your purpose in mind, no matter what I do. In Jesus' Name, Amen.

Lifted Reflections...

_____

_____

_____

_____

_____

_____

_____

_____

_____

_____

_____

_____

_____

_____

_____

_____

_____

I want to get life right

"For I know the plans I have for you," declares the LORD, "plans to prosper you and not to harm you, plans to give you hope and a future." - Jeremiah 29:11

He has plans to give us a hope and a future. He wants to prosper us. In order to get life right, we need to do our part and let Him do His. The challenge is understanding which part is ours and which part is His. This is why we must seek Him every day and talk to Him throughout the day. He takes us one step at a time. Learning to enjoy the process of walking the path with Him is essential. He has unexpected blessings and surprises awaiting us. He answers our prayers, but usually not at all in the way we expect it. We just need to remain obedient and magnify His name.

Are you following His plan for your life or your own? What does getting life right look like to you?

God, I want to get life right. Help me to continue to trust Your Word — the map You've provided to instruct me in living. Help me redeem the time I've lost from not following Your plan before today, and give me hope that You will light my path from this day forward. In Jesus' Name, Amen.

Lifted Reflections...

_____

_____

_____

_____

_____

_____

_____

_____

_____

_____

_____

_____

_____

_____

_____

_____

Ask & Receive

"However, as it is written: 'What no eye has seen, what no ear has heard, and what no human mind has conceived' — the things God has prepared for those who love him." - 1 Corinthians 2:9

I don't know about you, but I know that I want all the things God has prepared for me. I'm expecting to be most blessed by the One who loves me best. I'm still learning to ask Him for what my heart desires and part of this process is learning to feel worthy to make such requests. I have struggled with receiving for as long as I can remember. He is showing me how to grow in this area and receive with grace, knowing that He wants to bless me and sometimes those blessings will come through others that He places on my path. Remaining humble and centered on Him is essential for growth in this area of my life.

Are you ready to receive what God has prepared for you? Have you made any requests of Him lately?

God, thank you for loving me the way You do. I know my requests are small in Your eyes and I'm grateful that You plan to give me more than I ask for. I am patiently waiting to receive all that You have prepared for me. I am Your good and faithful daughter. In Jesus' Name, Amen.

Lifted Reflections...

_____

_____

_____

_____

_____

_____

_____

_____

_____

_____

_____

_____

_____

_____

_____

_____

_____

Shine Bright

"In the same way, let your light shine before others, that they may see your good deeds and glorify your Father in heaven." - Matthew 5:16

In this world we live in, the moment you step into your calling, you will be attacked, ridiculed and criticized. You will also be encouraged, loved and supported.

"So, because you are lukewarm—neither hot nor cold—I am about to spit you out of my mouth." - Revelations 3:16

This is a spiritual battle. There will be times you will feel His presence working in and through you...you will feel strong, loved and powerful beyond measure. There are also times that you will be tired and will need to renew your strength. Take time to rest and renew, but don't you dare stop shining your light. Don't you dare stop sharing your gift.

We need to see His love, light, strength and wisdom shining bright and strong through you. In a world where you can be anything, don't let the opinions of others drown your inner voice out, causing you to settle for less. Dare to be different, be you and be the change!

In what areas do you need to move away from being lukewarm so you can shine bright?

God, this world is filled with people who want me to conform to the ways of the world. Please give me the courage to shine Your light bright so that others can see that I will always choose You over everything. I want to please You with the way I live my life. I want to be hot in all that I do to honor and love You. Amen.

Lifted Reflections...

_____

_____

_____

_____

_____

_____

_____

_____

_____

_____

_____

_____

_____

_____

_____

_____

Dream big dreams

"'If you can'?" said Jesus. "Everything is possible for one who believes." - Mark 9:23

Dear God, help my children and I to continue to dream dreams that are too big for us to accomplish on our own. I want us to have Your purpose in mind, no matter what we do.

I'm ready to do whatever it takes to live my life according to Your plan, for I know You have called me by name and that all things are possible for the one who believes.

What dreams are you believing God for today?

God, as I seek You and Your will for my life, I ask that You make it clear which dreams are motivated by You. Please show me how to live less for me and more for You. In Jesus' Name, Amen.

Lifted Reflections...

_____

_____

_____

_____

_____

_____

_____

_____

_____

_____

_____

_____

_____

_____

_____

_____

_____

Rock & Redeemer

"May these words of my mouth and this meditation of my heart be pleasing in your sight, LORD, my Rock and my Redeemer." - Psalm 19:14

You are my rock and my redeemer. You know my purpose and you guide me towards it. I trust You and draw strength from You as I sit with You in prayer and meditation. Those who know me, know that I have their best interests in mind because You reside in me. You are my ultimate source. You give me energy and strength. I know my purpose and walk in it with confidence because You are my Rock and Redeemer.

What does this verse mean to you? What does it mean to you to have the meditation of your heart be pleasing in His sight?

God, search my heart and help me do the necessary work to get rid of anything that is not pleasing in Your eyes. I want a pure heart that is motivated by Your love. In Jesus' Name. I pray. Amen.

Lifted Reflections...

_____

_____

_____

_____

_____

_____

_____

_____

_____

_____

_____

_____

_____

_____

_____

_____

Obedient Faith

"For we live by faith, not by sight." - 2 Corinthians 5:7

The more I lean into Him, the more I learn to obey, hear, see, and do what He directs me to do. For someone with a strong personality like myself, it has taken serious work to get to this point. The more I am willing to submit and obey, the more beautiful the walk through life is with Him.

Today I am so blessed and completely thankful that, where I was once blind, I can now see the path that He reveals to me as I walk a Christ-centered life in total faith.

How do you know when you are living by faith and not by sight?

God, thank you for leading and strengthening my faith. Thank you for putting people on my path to support me as I walk by faith and not by sight. I ask that You continue to lift me higher as I take each new step in obedient faith with You. Amen.

Lifted Reflections...

_____

_____

_____

_____

_____

_____

_____

_____

_____

_____

_____

_____

_____

_____

_____

_____

A desire to please Him

"Put on the full armor of God, so that you can take your stand against the devil's schemes." - Ephesians 6:11

I have a heart filled with a desire to please Him. He fills me with His spirit each day so I have the strength, wisdom and discernment to live a good life by making wholesome choices that are aligned with His Word. He has a purpose and plan for each one of us and He doesn't do anything small. We often look to others for clarity about what it is we need to do. We need to resist that tendency to get the approval of people and look to Him, our Creator.

My life's purpose has become so incredibly clear the more I turn to Him. I love how He reveals each bold step as I walk with Him in surrendered obedience and faith. This new walk with Him is the most beautiful, abundant walk I have ever experienced. I'm fixing my eyes on Him and ignoring the noise of the world. The noise can be loud, especially as you take big steps in faith. What He has called each one of us to do is too important to let the noise take us off course. Live bold today as you take that next brave step in faith.

Are you living to please others or to please Him? What is the next brave step in faith that you need to take?

God, I have a desire to please You with how I live my life. I am ready to take the next brave step in faith that You are calling me to take. I am patiently awaiting Your divine guidance. In Jesus' Name, Amen.

Lifted Reflections...

_____

_____

_____

_____

_____

_____

_____

_____

_____

_____

_____

_____

_____

_____

_____

_____

_____

_____

Sin is sin

"If anyone, then, knows the good they ought to do and doesn't do it, it is sin for them." - James 4:17

We often think of sin as something more serious, or at least I did.

When I learned of this "ignoring" my heart kind of sin, that is when my life began to change for the better. This is how I, over time, got back to my most loving, authentic, true self.

When God puts something on our hearts to do and we ignore it, we are not only sinning against ourselves, we are also sinning against Him. When I learned this truth, my walk in obedience to Him got serious fast. I'm not messing with God. I used to be okay with sinning against myself, but now that I know when I sin against myself for the comfort of others, I am also sinning against Him. Nope. Not messing with Him. Not anymore. He is a good, loving and faithful Father, who wants to bless us abundantly.

Today, I'm so thankful for this new understanding, as I listen to my heart and do what He directs me to do each day. When I stay centered in His love, the path is revealed in a peaceful and deliberate manner, one glorious step at a time. By listening to Him I began the healing journey back to loving myself as the woman created in His image.

What are you being directed to do to stay centered in His love? Are you ignoring anything that you ought to do?

God, I desire to have such an intimate relationship with You that I know what to do the moment you whisper to me. Regardless of how loud life gets, I will listen for Your whisper every step of the way so that I can do all the good I ought to do in Your name. Amen.

Lifted Reflections...

_____

_____

_____

_____

_____

_____

_____

_____

_____

_____

_____

_____

_____

_____

_____

_____

_____

Unspeakable hardships

"You are my hiding place; you will protect me from trouble and surround me with songs of deliverance." - Psalm 32:7

Throughout life we experience unspeakable hardships that hit us from out of nowhere and rock us to the core. It is during these times that we experience being surrounded with songs of deliverance. Take rest in Him. Be still and know that He will carry you through. I've witnessed and experienced what faith in Christ will do. Stay centered in His love, lean into Him and experience a perfect peace that only He can provide as you ride out the emotional waves of the brutal storm. You are loved beyond anything you can ever imagine. Receive His love. Let Him in.

"There is a time for everything, and a season for every activity under the heavens: a time to be born and a time to die, a time to plant and a time to uproot, a time to kill and a time to heal, a time to tear down and a time to build, a time to weep and a time to laugh, a time to mourn and a time to dance, a time to scatter stones and a time to gather them, a time to embrace and a time to refrain from embracing, a time to search and a time to give up, a time to keep and a time to throw away, a time to tear and a time to mend, a time to be silent and a time to speak, a time to love and a time to hate, a time for war and a time for peace." - Ecclesiastes 3:1-8

How has God shown up for you during an unspeakable hardship? What does unspeakable hardship mean to you?

God, thank you for bringing me close and carrying me through the hardships that I have faced in life. As I look back, I can see the good that You have done during each of the times that I hit rock bottom. Thank you for loving me through it all. I'm grateful to know I can count on You all the days of my life and that nothing takes You by surprise. Amen.

Lifted Reflections...

_____

_____

_____

_____

_____

_____

_____

_____

_____

_____

_____

_____

_____

_____

_____

_____

_____

_____

Mourning & Dancing

"He gives strength to the weary and increases the power of the weak." - Isaiah 40:29

"Blessed are those who mourn, for they will be comforted." - Matthew 5:4

Today I ask for renewed strength, peace, wisdom, unconditional love and forgiveness.

At 3:00 I go to court to receive my official name change back to my maiden name, Fulp. After 18 years of being McMahon, this day is a day that I take pause in, reflect upon and seek His love to understand and continue the necessary healing process. It is with mixed emotions that I will legally be Mary Teresa Fulp again. My parents taught me what marriage is and should be. I fell way short and have experienced a great deal of grief for doing so. This is not how I expected my life to go. I value marriage and love according to God's purpose for it. I also value and own my story, my choices, the good times and the bad...all of it. I'm thankful for where I am today and I ask for God's love to carry my children and I through the emotional waves that are surfacing as a result of this name change, of this life change.

What do you need from God today?

God, may I always remember to make my requests known to You and then wait expectantly for You to deliver on Your promises. Amen

Lifted Reflections...

_____

_____

_____

_____

_____

_____

_____

_____

_____

_____

_____

_____

_____

_____

_____

_____

_____

_____

Challenges we face

"And we know that in all things God works for the good of those who love him, who have been called according to his purpose." - Romans 8:28

The challenges we face in life are designed for our benefit and growth. We need to embrace all the circumstances He allows in our lives and remain centered in faith, trusting Him to bring good out of them. Let the feelings of fear and stress be indicators of the need to spend time with Him. Our needs become the doors that lead us to great dependence on Him. For when we are weak, then we are strong if we turn to Him.

Heavenly Father, I thank you for being with me in good times and in bad. I'm learning to lean into your love more and more. I pray that I continue to seek you at all times, that I keep you in Your proper place in my life. Thank you for never leaving my presence, even when I leave yours. Now that I know better I will do better. I will continue to choose faith over fear and You above all else.

What challenges are you currently facing and how are they designed for your growth?

God, please give us the wisdom to see the deeper meaning in the challenges we face, so we can understand on a spiritual level how they are preparing us for our purpose and are designed for our growth. May we grow in trust and intimacy with You as we press on, knowing we need You every step of the way. In Jesus' Name, I pray. Amen.

Lifted Reflections...

_____

_____

_____

_____

_____

_____

_____

_____

_____

_____

_____

_____

_____

_____

_____

_____

_____

_____

When I am weak

"Each time he said, 'My grace is all you need. My power works best in weakness.' So now I am glad to boast about my weaknesses, so that the power of Christ can work through me." - 2 Corinthians 12:9

I'm grateful for my weaknesses that have brought me closer to Him. I now know it is He that makes me strong. What an incredible blessing it is to understand that I can do all things with and through Him.

I am known by my close family and friends for being a strong and independent woman. This has been both a blessing and a challenge for me throughout life. I am on a path to understanding who I am and how much I need Jesus in my life to bring out the very best in me. He created me to be a woman who can do many things, but not all things. I can only do all things through Him who gives me strength.

What weaknesses have brought you closer to Him?

God, thank You for loving me the way You do. Take all of me — my weaknesses and my strengths — to use for Your glory. In Jesus' Name, Amen.

Lifted Reflections...

_____

_____

_____

_____

_____

_____

_____

_____

_____

_____

_____

_____

_____

_____

_____

_____

_____

_____

Everything is possible

"'If you can'?" said Jesus. "Everything is possible for one who believes." - Mark 9:23

If you put your disbelief aside, roll up your sleeves, take some risks, and totally go for it, you'll wake up one day and realize you're living the kind of life you've always dreamed of. Our world needs more believers that live with passion for their purpose!

In what way do you need to totally go for it in your life? What does this verse mean to you?

God, search my mind and heart to get rid of any unbelief I have that is interfering with everything that is possible. Amen.

Lifted Reflections...

_____

_____

_____

_____

_____

_____

_____

_____

_____

_____

_____

_____

_____

_____

_____

_____

_____

Seek His face

"Look to the Lord and his strength; seek his face always."
- Psalm 105:4

Regardless of what is going on or how I feel, I choose to seek Him. He provides clarity and strength in the midst of every situation. With Him, anything and everything is possible. Believe and walk in faith today!

What does it mean to believe and walk in faith in this very moment in your life?

God, I look to You and seek Your face. I know that I am who I am in and through You. As I seek Your face, I ask You to lift me higher into the divine purpose you have for my life. In Jesus' Name, Amen.

Lifted Reflections...

_____

_____

_____

_____

_____

_____

_____

_____

_____

_____

_____

_____

_____

_____

_____

_____

When I wake up

"You did not choose me, but I chose you and appointed you so that you might go and bear fruit — fruit that will last — and so that whatever you ask in my name the Father will give you." - John 15:16

When I wake up, I ask God to show me what He needs me to do today and give me the courage and strength to do it. He always delivers and provides such incredible clarity as I walk in the path of his light and love. He reveals the next step at just the right time. When we stay centered in Christ, we don't have to live in the past or the future, we get to thoroughly enjoy living in the now.

What do you do when you wake up? Are you starting your day with Him?

God, I want to bear fruit that will last and seed that will multiply to advance Your Kingdom on earth during my short time here. I want to live and leave a legacy that matters. I ask this in Your name. Amen.

Lifted Reflections...

_____

_____

_____

_____

_____

_____

_____

_____

_____

_____

_____

_____

_____

_____

_____

_____

_____

My Daughter

"Every good and perfect gift is from above, coming down from the Father of the heavenly lights, who does not change like shifting shadows." - James 1:17

As a mother, I had always wanted a daughter. After having two amazing boys, I began to accept the idea that I would never have a mother, daughter relationship like I have with my own mother. It was with great sadness that I began to move to the next phase in life. In my mind I was done having kids and it must not have been part of my life's plan. When I least expected it, I learned I was pregnant again. I also learned another valuable lesson about who God is and how He works. He always delivers in His way and in His time.

Today I give thanks and praise to our Heavenly Father for blessing my life abundantly, over and over again. He is a good and faithful Father.

How has God shown up in your life when you least expected it? When has He moved in your life to bless you abundantly, beyond anything you imagined? How did you respond?

God, thank you for blessing me abundantly. May I learn to expect You to deliver on Your promises rather than giving up hope when it doesn't happen in my way or in my time. Your timing is always perfect and You are rarely early. I know during the wait that You are preparing me to receive Your blessing. I trust You. In Jesus' Name, Amen.

Lifted Reflections...

_____

_____

_____

_____

_____

_____

_____

_____

_____

_____

_____

_____

_____

_____

_____

_____

_____

_____

What we think about we bring about

"Finally, brothers and sisters, whatever is true, whatever is noble, whatever is right, whatever is pure, whatever is lovely, whatever is admirable—if anything is excellent or praiseworthy—think about such things." - Philippians 4:8

What we think about, we bring about. Cast down all thoughts that do not align with God's Word. The truth of His love sets us free. Manifest the good things God has for us by thinking and meditating on the truth of His word.

What are you thinking about? If the things you think about most often were to manifest in your life, would you be happy with the outcome?

God, help me quickly rebuke any thoughts that are not praiseworthy and excellent in Your eyes. In Jesus' Name, Amen.

Lifted Reflections...

_____

_____

_____

_____

_____

_____

_____

_____

_____

_____

_____

_____

_____

_____

_____

_____

_____

_____

We must hear & do

He replied, "Blessed rather are those who hear the word of God and obey it." - Luke 11:28

We must hear and do. Our world needs more believers that do. It is our job to put into practice the work that God has called us to do. It isn't always easy, so we must seek His strength and have the courage to obey by acting on what we hear from Him. He will reveal the next step as we walk in obedience.

Have you ever agreed to humbly obey God when you would rather not? What fruit have you seen from your obedience?

God, in my flesh I'm likely to disregard your voice and go my own way. Give me a heart that longs to humbly obey You no matter how I feel. In Jesus' Name, I pray. Amen.

Lifted Reflections...

_____

_____

_____

_____

_____

_____

_____

_____

_____

_____

_____

_____

_____

_____

_____

_____

_____

Learn to trust Him

"But blessed is the one who trusts in the Lord, whose confidence is in him." - Jeremiah 17:7

Trust can be challenging, especially when we have been hurt by people we've loved and trusted in the past. God loves us unconditionally and is the One we can put our complete trust in. He will always come through for us. Lean into Him and learn to trust His ways. He is a way maker and a promise keeper.

How can I learn to trust in God with all my heart? What is one thing I need to trust God to do in my life today, that I can't do on my own?

God, I want to be a person who trusts in You wholeheartedly and stands firm in my faith regardless of what I see. Develop that deeper trust in me. I want to trust You more and more each day. I need help releasing my control to You. In Jesus' Name, Amen.

Lifted Reflections...

_____

_____

_____

_____

_____

_____

_____

_____

_____

_____

_____

_____

_____

_____

_____

_____

_____

_____

Called out of the darkness & into the light

"But you are a chosen people, a royal priesthood, a holy nation, God's special possession, that you may declare the praises of him who called you out of darkness into his wonderful light." - 1 Peter 2:9

What a beautiful day it is when He calls us out of the darkness and into the light. Today I take pause to meditate and reflect on His love. I thank you, Jesus, for surrounding me with people who embody such radiant love and light. My cup runneth over to have such loving servant hearts surrounding me in my daily walk of living a life filled with faith, hope and love.

It brings me so much joy to witness God working in the lives of my own children and family members as they turn to Him and seek a more intimate relationship with Him. It is amazing to see how He takes each one of us as we are and develops our faith in such an intimate and authentic manner. He knows what each one of us needs and meets us where we are, no matter how near or far, no matter how old or young. He loves to love us.

Have you experienced being called out of the darkness and into His light? How can you remain in His light when you are surrounded by darkness?

God, I want to armor up with all that You are so that I can be a light in the darkness. I know there are many people who are stuck in a dark place and need Your love to lift them higher. Use me, God, to be an instrument of Your loving presence in this dark world. Amen.

Lifted Reflections...

_____

_____

_____

_____

_____

_____

_____

_____

_____

_____

_____

_____

_____

_____

_____

_____

_____

Painful preparation

"God will strengthen you with his own great power so that you will not give up when troubles come, but you will be patient." - Colossians 1:11

Thank You for showing me that You're more interested in preparing me than keeping me comfortable. I do not always enjoy the preparation. I admit that sometimes I'd rather get exactly what I want when I want it. When I can't see the path I trust You will reveal the next step at exactly the right time. I trust in Your ways over mine. I know Your ways bring out the best in me for the good of myself and others. I know I can trust You when You allow me to be placed into situations I would rather avoid. I know that with pressure and time You are shaping me to do what you've called me to do. I'm grateful that You are strengthening me during this season in life. I know the work You're doing in me is good. I turn to You at all times so I can remain centered in You, trusting Your purpose for my life and remaining patient with the process of, sometimes painful, preparation.

How have you experienced painful preparation in your life? How has it helped shape you into the person you are today?

God, I know You desire to make me more like You. Thank you for shaping me into a stronger person with a greater purpose during this painful pruning process that you are taking me through. Amen

Lifted Reflections...

_____

_____

_____

_____

_____

_____

_____

_____

_____

_____

_____

_____

_____

_____

_____

_____

_____

_____

You were born to make a difference

"Before I formed you in the womb I knew you, before you were born I set you apart; I appointed you as a prophet to the nations." - Jeremiah 1:5

You were born to make a difference. It's time to be the unapologetic person God created you to be from the very beginning. He has special plans for each one of us. We need to act with courage to be the truest version of ourselves, the person we were before this fear-based world got ahold of us. Be bold and live loved. We need to see everyone rise strong by trusting God and doing good.

How are you using your unique and special gift to make a difference? Are you living your truth according to the person God created you to be?

God, give me the courage to live my life according to the person You created me to be. When I am pressured to be like others, give me the strength to honor You and truly be set apart. In Jesus' Name, Amen.

Lifted Reflections...

_____

_____

_____

_____

_____

_____

_____

_____

_____

_____

_____

_____

_____

_____

_____

_____

_____

He always comes through

"And God is able to give you more than you need, so that you will always have all you need for yourselves and more than enough for every good cause." - 2 Corinthians 9:8

He always comes through in His way and in His time. I am learning to trust Him with everything in my life. As I do this, I receive His perfect peace. There have been times in the past that I would worry and try to fix or figure out everything on my own. I now know how much He loves to take care of me and provide for my every need. I'm learning to let go of the need to control and, instead, receive from Him. I know I must continue to trust, do good and act on the things that He places on my heart. His grace is such a beautiful blessing. Today I choose to trust and walk in His perfect peace.

How has God come through for you in the past? What do you need God to do in order to come through for you now or in the near future?

God, I am asking You to cover all of my needs and give me more than enough for every good cause You place on my heart to support. I am ready to live full out for all that You have called me to do. I need You now more than ever to be my strength and provider. In Jesus' Name, Amen.

Lifted Reflections...

Show me what you need me to do today

"When He, the Spirit of truth, has come, He will guide you into all truth." - John 16:13

Every morning I ask God to show me what I need to do today and give me the courage to do it. Walking in the Spirit is an amazing experience, especially when you realize the impact on yourself and others is something you could never have done on your own. Trust and act today. We need all believers to do the work they are called to do. The truth sets us free and free, is a beautiful place to be!

How are you living your life each day? Are you asking God to show you what He needs you to do?

God, thank you for guiding me to do Your work each day. Sometimes it is obvious what You need me to do and other times it isn't. I ask that You slow me down and convict me when I'm living in my own flesh, so that I can see what You need me to do and not what I think I should do. In Jesus' Name, Amen.

Lifted Reflections...

_____

_____

_____

_____

_____

_____

_____

_____

_____

_____

_____

_____

_____

_____

_____

_____

_____

One of a kind

"So in Christ we, though many, form one body, and each member belongs to all the others." - Romans 12:5

We each have a call on our life. We are one of a kind and have our own unique gift to develop and share. He has a different call for each one of us. None of us are capable of doing all the work, but we are capable and called to do our part masterfully. We are all needed and together we can ignite a beautiful masterpiece of love in this world as we share His love and light with others while we are walking faithfully in our purpose.

What makes you one of a kind? How can you develop your gift further to glorify and honor God?

God, I want to do the thing You have called me to do with excellence. I do not want to do many things, but the one thing You have called me to do well. I ask that You develop and strengthen my spiritual gift as I grow in excellence to honor and serve You. In Jesus' Name, Amen.

Lifted Reflections...

Keep your word truthful & positive

"Behold, You desire truth in the inward parts, And in the hidden *part* You will make me to know wisdom." - Psalm 51:6

Keep your word truthful and positive. When we speak the positive truth, we give life to ourselves and one another. People crave the truth, but we aren't always ready to hear it. When we seek the truth and live it in love each day, we begin to set ourselves and those in our presence free. We can all benefit from living and speaking the positive truth today. What we speak, we give life to. Let's give life to the truth of what we need more of in our lives. More faith, love, understanding, forgiveness, hope, encouragement, trust, strength, peace and truth.

How can you be more truthful and positive with the words you speak?

God, the truth of Your word sets us free. Give me wisdom to know when I'm being deceived or led astray with the lies of the enemy. Reveal the truth as I seek it and give me the courage to always speak the positive truth to myself and others. In Jesus' Name, I pray. Amen.

Lifted Reflections...

_____

_____

_____

_____

_____

_____

_____

_____

_____

_____

_____

_____

_____

_____

_____

_____

_____

_____

Meditate on the Word

"If you believe, you will receive whatever you ask for in prayer." - Matthew 21:22

This is a verse that I choose to meditate on today. What does it mean to believe, to truly trust and believe in what you pray for when all you have is a prayer? How do you prepare your heart and mind to receive when your prayer is answered? Sometimes we will pray for a few days and receive an answer in a way that looks exactly like what we prayed for. Other times our prayers may take years to come to pass and when they do, they are often answered in a time and manner in which we could not even begin to imagine on our own. What must we do in the meantime? BELIEVE. We must hold fast to our faith, obey God and believe. We must believe He will answer and then prepare our hearts and minds to receive.

What are you believing God for? What have you asked for in prayer?

God, forgive me for the times I struggle to believe. Your truth permeates every single layer of my life. I believe in You and need You to help me overcome any unbelief I still have inside of me that I may not even be aware of. I need You to reveal behaviors and patterns that I have developed over time that serve as barriers to my belief in You to do all things. In Jesus' Name, Amen.

Lifted Reflections...

_____

_____

_____

_____

_____

_____

_____

_____

_____

_____

_____

_____

_____

_____

_____

_____

_____

He directs our steps

"A man's heart plans his way, but the Lord directs his steps."
- Proverbs 16:9

This is the verse I chose when I got baptized last year. I learned my lessons the hard way. I definitely know how to make my own plans, and for many years was doing so without seeking God. I'm now learning to walk in the Spirit as He guides my steps each and every day. Lord show me what you need me to do today and give me the courage to do it. Give me the awareness to see and hear You as I go about doing the work You have called me to do. Thank you for giving me eyes to see, ears to hear, and a heart to feel Your presence. Where I was once blind, now I see. Praise God! You brought me out of the darkness and into Your glorious light. Thank you, Jesus!

How are you allowing God to direct your steps?

God, I thank You for directing my steps. The more I seek You, the more clearly I hear from You. I do not want to go down my own path. I have done that long enough. I want to be with You on the path You have for my life from this day forward. In Jesus' Name, Amen.

Lifted Reflections...

_____

_____

_____

_____

_____

_____

_____

_____

_____

_____

_____

_____

_____

_____

_____

_____

_____

Build people up

"This is how the LORD responds: 'If you return to me, I will restore you so you can continue to serve me. If you speak good words rather than worthless ones, you will be my spokesman. You must influence them; do not let them influence you!'" - Jeremiah 15:19

We are called to build people up, to speak life into others. When we speak the positive truth, we encourage others to rise to the level they have within themselves. When we judge and criticize others, we become sad and miserable ourselves. What we sow, we reap. We need to shut down toxic conversations immediately so we aren't giving life to the hurtful behaviors and words of others. Look for ways to build others up today with the uplifting words you speak and actions you take. We rise by lifting others!

How are you using your gifts to build people up?

God, I desire to please You with the words I speak and the actions I take. I will use my gifts and abilities to be the spokesperson You have called me to be. I will build people up with Your loving truth. Amen.

Lifted Reflections...

Do everything in love

"Be on your guard; stand firm in the faith; be courageous; be strong. Do everything in love." - 1 Corinthians 16:13-14

Each day as we put on the love of Jesus and walk in the Spirit, it is absolutely beautiful to see what He does through us to bless others. In giving, we truly receive the best gift of all. The gift of His love is a gift that money can't buy and words can't quite describe. Some gifts are too precious and priceless to define. They are only designed to be felt with a direct explosive, radiant shot to the heart.

What does it mean to you to do everything in love?

God, I strive to do everything in love. I know I fall short at times and I am thankful that You humble me when do. I ask that You continue to purify my heart so I can love like You do. In Jesus' Name, Amen.

Lifted Reflections...

_____

_____

_____

_____

_____

_____

_____

_____

_____

_____

_____

_____

_____

_____

_____

_____

_____

_____

True Happiness

"You will seek me and find me when you seek me with all your heart." - Jeremiah 29:13

True happiness comes from the pursuit of God. I was the person who longed for inner and true happiness for so long. I even facilitated a college class on happiness with the Happy books, including "Even Happier: A Gratitude Journal for Daily Joy and Lasting Fulfillment" by Tal Ben-Shahar. It wasn't until I began to open my Bible and seek the Word of God with all my heart that I learned to understand true happiness. I have found that while I was a person in pursuit of happiness, I was actually a woman in desperate need of God Himself.

What does true happiness mean to you and how do you get it?

God, I see so many people in the world who seek happiness from temporary things. I do not want to be a woman who seeks instant gratification to make me happy. I want to be a woman who seeks You with my whole heart for everlasting peace and happiness. You are my source. Amen.

Lifted Reflections...

_____

_____

_____

_____

_____

_____

_____

_____

_____

_____

_____

_____

_____

_____

_____

_____

_____

_____

Serving God

"I will give thanks to you, Lord, with all my heart; I will tell of all your wonderful deeds." - Psalm 9:1

I will strive to see every part of my day as an opportunity to serve God with all my heart. I will choose to give thanks and show gratitude in the moment. I will limit distractions and keep my eyes on Him. I know He is directing my every step and is doing it for His namesake. I am so thankful I get to honor and serve Him each and every day.

What do you give thanks to God for and how do you share the good news of His wonderful deeds with others?

God, it is my goal to give thanks to You all the days of my life no matter how I feel. I thank You for loving me the way You do and giving me a heart that delights in serving others. You are an awesome Father. Amen.

Lifted Reflections...

_____

_____

_____

_____

_____

_____

_____

_____

_____

_____

_____

_____

_____

_____

_____

_____

_____

_____

_____

Pure joy

"Consider it pure joy, my brothers and sisters, whenever you face trials of many kinds, because you know that the testing of your faith produces perseverance. Let perseverance finish its work so that you may be mature and complete, not lacking anything." - James 1:2-4

I consider it pure joy to know that I can do nothing of value without God. I am learning through the trials in life just how much I need His love. He offers me a perfect peace and pure joy just as another storm develops. He carries me through it all. What a beautiful name it is, the name of Jesus Christ our King.

What does this verse mean to you? Have you faced a trial of any kind that you were able to see the deeper level of perseverance that was being produced? Were you able to consider it pure joy?

God, I want to trust the deeper meaning of the trials I face and consider them pure joy knowing that the testing of my faith produces perseverance, that I will be lacking in nothing when Your work is complete. In Jesus' Name, Amen.

Lifted Reflections...

_____

_____

_____

_____

_____

_____

_____

_____

_____

_____

_____

_____

_____

_____

_____

_____

_____

Do Good & Trust God

"Wait for the Lord; be strong, and let your heart take courage; wait for the Lord!" - Psalm 27:14

Do good and trust God. Do good and trust God. Do good and Trust God. Do what? And trust who? All day long!

I have found that this is the best advice, especially during uncertain times. When I'm in a season of waiting and I don't know what to do, I do this and it works every time.

How do you wait for the Lord? What do you do while you are waiting on Him?

God, as I wait on You, I will continue to do good and trust in You and Your promises. In Jesus' Name, Amen.

Lifted Reflections...

_____

_____

_____

_____

_____

_____

_____

_____

_____

_____

_____

_____

_____

_____

_____

_____

Love transcends barriers

"The person without the Spirit does not accept the things that come from the Spirit of God but considers them foolishness, and cannot understand them because they are discerned only through the Spirit." - 1 Corinthians 2:14

This is definitely something I understand from my own experience. I have lived with and without, which makes me that much more aware of this journey and how important it is, regardless of one's own understanding. I strive to do all things in love. Loving actions transcend all barriers. We are here to love and be loved. Let God's love shine on others through you. We can be set apart and different, while we love others more and care less about how they view us.

Are you living in the Spirit or in the flesh most often? How do you know? What does this verse mean to you? Have you experienced being considered foolish by others when you are being obedient to God?

God, I want to live a life that pleases You. I ask that You give me the discernment to know when I am motivated by the wrong things. I want to consistently be motivated by serving You with a pure heart. In Jesus' Name, Amen.

Lifted Reflections...

_____

_____

_____

_____

_____

_____

_____

_____

_____

_____

_____

_____

_____

_____

_____

_____

_____

_____

Centered on Him

"Be alert and of sober mind. Your enemy the devil prowls around like a roaring lion looking for someone to devour." - 1 Peter 5:8

We need to be well-balanced so we can remain centered and strong. Today I will strive to find balance in all that I do. I will work and rest. I will take care of one task at a time and I will do each task at a peaceful pace. I will seek joy and meaning in all that I do. I will find balance so I can remain centered in God's love.

What does it mean to be alert and of sober mind? What do you do to remain centered on Him?

God, I am at my best when I am well-balanced with You at the center of all I do. Help me remain alert, centered and strong in You. Amen.

Lifted Reflections...

_____

_____

_____

_____

_____

_____

_____

_____

_____

_____

_____

_____

_____

_____

_____

_____

_____

I can through Christ

"I can do all things through Christ who strengthens me." - Philippians 4:13

The difference between I can and I can't is Christ. When we realize this, we are filled with His strength to do things we could never humanly do on our own. I am so grateful for this new understanding. Life can be so hard at times, but we are not meant to carry it all on our own. Seek Him and He will strengthen you.

"If a soldier demands that you carry his gear for a mile, carry it two miles." - Matthew 5:41

When was the last time you did something that you knew you could only have done because of Him?

God, I can go the extra mile with and through You. You are my strength. When I'm tempted to say I can't, I will instead say I can through Christ who strengthens me. In Jesus' Name, Amen.

Lifted Reflections...

_____

_____

_____

_____

_____

_____

_____

_____

_____

_____

_____

_____

_____

_____

_____

_____

_____

_____

Be the Gift

"A good name is more desirable than great riches; to be esteemed is better than silver or gold." - Proverbs 22:1

Who are you? Be the gift that you were created to be. Whatever you are meant to be, you possess it now. Unleash your divine presence from the inside out. We need you. We need the gift that you are. You are more precious than silver & gold.

I am Mary Teresa. I am here to add value.

Who do you know that has a good name? What are the qualities of their character that you most admire?

God, I am grateful to know people who live to give and make our world a better place. Thank you for surrounding me with people who have a "good name" because they genuinely love You and live their lives with integrity. In Jesus' Name, Amen.

Lifted Reflections...

_____

_____

_____

_____

_____

_____

_____

_____

_____

_____

_____

_____

_____

_____

_____

_____

Continue to do good

"Trust in the LORD and do good; dwell in the land and enjoy safe pasture." - Psalm 37:3

It is amazing what happens when you turn to God and consistently do good. Doing what is good can be difficult at times, but the time is always right to do good. Remain in faith and trust God. The seeds we sow, grow...so do good and keep doing good. No matter what you are facing, continue to do good and trust God. He will work it all out. He will handle the rest and give you sweet rest!

What good are you doing consistently?

God, I love doing good in Your name and I'm ready to do it on a larger scale to honor and glorify You. Amen.

Lifted Reflections...

_____

_____

_____

_____

_____

_____

_____

_____

_____

_____

_____

_____

_____

_____

_____

_____

_____

Hope

"Yes, my soul, find rest in God; my hope comes from him."
- Psalm 62:5

My hope comes from the Lord. My renewed strength comes from Him. When life feels overwhelming. When those mountains seem to be in surmountable, know that He will provide a way in His time. Rest and remain steadfast. Choose faith over fear. Choose faith over feelings.

Today I choose gratitude for all the good that He is doing and has done.

What or who gives you hope?

God, You are my hope and today I am grateful for all the good You are doing and have already done. Our world needs more of You. May we grow an army of believers who give hope to the hopeless. In Jesus' Name, Amen.

Lifted Reflections...

I need Him

"Those who look to Him are radiant; their faces are never covered with shame." - Psalm 34:5

I am reminded quickly, how much I need Him every time I look away. His unconditional love is a gift I treasure as I strive to rise strong each time I fall short. Today I choose to keep my eyes fixed on Him and pause to seek help from the Holy Spirit as I go about my day. My help comes from the Lord. Thank you Jesus for giving me another chance to get it right with and through You.

When do you need Him? How often do you seek Him? Do you notice a pattern of when and how often you seek Him?

God, I need You all the time. When I feel guilt or shame knocking at my door, I know it's the enemy trying to get in. All I need to do to cast down the lies is look to You for Your radiant covering and speak Your Word to counter the lies. In Jesus' Name, Amen.

Lifted Reflections...

_____

_____

_____

_____

_____

_____

_____

_____

_____

_____

_____

_____

_____

_____

_____

_____

_____

Be a vessel of His love

"Whoever claims to live in Him must live as Jesus did."
- 1 John 2:6

Be a vessel of His loving presence. When we choose to put on love and get out in the world to share it, He will show us what to do and where to go. We must be ready for Him to surprise us with the love He wants to pour out on others through us. Trust His divine guidance and act on it. He needs us to be vessels of His loving presence.

How can I show up today as the loving face of Jesus in the lives of those who cross my path? What did Jesus do that we can learn from and live out as we walk in a faith-centered life?

God, I ask You to show me what You need me to do today and give me the strength and courage to do it. When people see me, I want them to see You. In Jesus' Name, I pray. Amen.

Lifted Reflections...

Pray More Worry Less

"Do not be anxious about anything, but in everything by prayer and supplication with thanksgiving let your requests be made known to God. And the peace of God, which surpasses all understanding, will guard your hearts and your minds in Christ Jesus." - Philippians 4:6-7

We do not need to worry about anything! God's got us. When we are busy and trying to do too much on our own, we begin to feel overwhelmed, confused and anxious. When this happens, immediately turn to Him and invite Him to be involved in everything. He does not want us to do it on our own. He loves it when we lean into Him. He loves it when we need Him. He brings us a perfect peace when we stay in His presence.

How often do you worry or get anxious about things? What is your immediate response when you begin to worry? Do you turn to prayer?

God, when I begin to worry or become anxious I want to instinctively and immediately turn to prayer. I want to get so good at doing this that I do it without even thinking and get to a place in my life where I truly worry about nothing because I give it all to You in prayer. In Jesus' Name, Amen.

Lifted Reflections...

Times of Trouble

"Fear not, for I am with you; be not dismayed, for I am your God. I will strengthen you, Yes, I will help you, I will uphold you with My righteous right hand." - Isaiah 41:10

During the times I have trouble sleeping and a hard time getting out of bed to face another busy day, I struggle to seek His face. These are the times I know I need to push through and get up and seek Him hard, knowing that the light of His love shines on me continually. I need to trust in Him at all times. Today I will shift my focus to His love and radiant presence. I will pause continually and say, "Jesus I need you. I can't do this on my own."

I will fear not, because I know He is with me.

What do you do in times of trouble?

God, in times of trouble I will seek You first. I choose to replace bad habits with good and healthy habits. I want to seek You first, not people or things, for answers that only You can provide. In Jesus' Name, Amen.

Lifted Reflections...

His unwavering Love

"Cast all your anxiety on him because he cares for you."
- 1 Peter 5:7

I am so grateful for sleep, good friends, family and God's consistent and unwavering love. Today I am exhausted, but I have coffee and the Holy Spirit to give me the energy I need to have an amazing day. Yes, an amazing day. There is no room for it to be anything less than the best He has to offer. He calls me out of the dark and into His glorious light.

I hope you can cast your anxiety to Him and join me in having an amazing day basking in His love and light!

What are you grateful for today?

God, every time I begin to have anxiety or find myself feeling unworthy, I will immediately turn to You in gratitude and prayer. I will think about all the good things that You are doing each and every day and make my requests known to You. In Jesus' Name, Amen.

Lifted Reflections...

_____

_____

_____

_____

_____

_____

_____

_____

_____

_____

_____

_____

_____

_____

_____

_____

_____

_____

Continue to show me

The King will reply, 'Truly I tell you, whatever you did for one of the least of these brothers and sisters of mine, you did for me.' - Matthew 25:40

Lord I ask that You continue to show me all the ways You need me to be a vessel of Your love and compassion in the lives of others. When the path appears dark and uncertain, I will trust You to light the way for each next step I take. I know that Your way is the only way for me and my loved ones. I thank You for directing my path and giving me the strength to be there for those who need Your love. Forgive me for the times I fall short and give me the courage to stand strong in Your presence each time the enemy tries to take me off course. I choose You over and over and over again. I choose You.

What do you need God to reveal to you so that you can grow stronger in Him?

God, I love it when You reveal Your ways to me. I feel like a child again excited for the next big adventure You are taking me on. I love to give and receive Your love. Continue to show me what You need me to do and what I need to put my trust in You to do. In Jesus' Name, Amen.

Lifted Reflections...

_____

_____

_____

_____

_____

_____

_____

_____

_____

_____

_____

_____

_____

_____

_____

_____

_____

_____

Starting my day in the Word

"Be alert and of sober mind. Your enemy the devil prowls around like a roaring lion looking for someone to devour." - 1 Peter 5:8

I've come to understand the importance of starting my day in the Word. I know the difference when I do and when I don't. I am beginning to understand how the enemy works. I will do my part to put on the full armor of God no matter how I'm feeling so that I can remain steadfast and centered in His love. It has been a battle lately and I'm determined to stand my ground by making good choices, choosing faith and staying balanced.

How do you start and end your day? How do you prepare yourself for the attacks of the enemy?

God, I have good habits formed to start my day with You. I need Your help to develop strong habits to end my day with You as well. Please help me develop good habits at the end of my day so that I can always rest in Your perfect peace. In Jesus' Name, Amen.

Lifted Reflections...

_____

_____

_____

_____

_____

_____

_____

_____

_____

_____

_____

_____

_____

_____

_____

_____

_____

The Truth Will Set You Free

"Instead, speaking the truth in love, we will grow to become in every respect the mature body of him who is the head, that is, Christ." - Ephesians 4:15

The truth will set you free. Be impeccable with your word. There is great power in speaking the truth in love. Be a person others can count on to always speak the truth, no matter how hard or uncomfortable it may be. Let the Holy Spirit guide you in the timing and delivery so that when you speak the truth it can be received and truly heard. We need more people to act with courage when it comes to speaking their authentic truth. Be courageous today and say what needs to be said in love.

How can the truth set you free? What is it that you've been hiding or holding back and how can you set yourself free by speaking and living the truth?

God, I am a truth seeker and speaker. I want to be known as someone who is consistent in living and speaking the truth in love. Thank you for showing me all the hidden areas where the truth needs to be shared in order to set myself and others free. I ask that You continue to guide me with Your loving truth. In Jesus' Name, Amen.

Lifted Reflections...

_____

_____

_____

_____

_____

_____

_____

_____

_____

_____

_____

_____

_____

_____

_____

Guard your heart

"Peace I leave with you; my peace I give you. I do not give to you as the world gives. Do not let your hearts be troubled and do not be afraid." - John 14:27

Do not let your heart be troubled and do not be afraid. As one of my good friends said to me, "fear is a sin." God did not give us a spirit of fear, He gave us a spirit of power, love and sound mind. When you find yourself in a place of fear, cast it down immediately and turn to God. Ask Him to give you the perfect peace only He can give. His ways don't always make sense. We must have faith and believe in Him through it all. Cast down fear and cling to faith. God is preparing and protecting us for something better than we can ever begin to imagine on our own. Let go and let God!

How's your heart today? Do you have anything on your heart that you need to let go of and give to God?

God, when I think about how awesome You are, I am overwhelmed. You do not give as the world gives and for that I am so incredibly grateful. You did not give me a spirit of fear, but of power, love and sound mind. In Jesus' Name, Amen.

Lifted Reflections...

His ways are higher

"I will instruct you and teach you in the way you should go; I will counsel you with my loving eye on you." - Psalm 32:8

He will guide us along the best pathway for our life. His ways are higher than our own. Learning to lean on Him and live in the moment is a challenge at times, but one worth pursuing. He will guide us along the BEST pathway for our life. He wants to give us the very best. Live loved today and let God bring His best your way!

What do you need to do today to pursue His best for you?

God, I know I get in my own way at times and I know Your ways are so much higher than my own. Today, I choose to get out of the way and receive the best You have for me. In Jesus' Name, I pray. Amen.

Lifted Reflections...

_____

_____

_____

_____

_____

_____

_____

_____

_____

_____

_____

_____

_____

_____

_____

_____

_____

Be a Giver

"In everything I did, I showed you that by this kind of hard work we must help the weak, remembering the words the Lord Jesus himself said: 'It is more blessed to give than to receive.'" - Acts 20:35

I am a giver and always have been. I am now learning ways to give without overspending my budget. During the holiday season, we can feel pressured by society to give to others in a way that is not in line with the true meaning of Christmas. Christmas is about Christ. Let's spend less and love more this year. My family will receive the love of Jesus and learn more about the true meaning of Christmas. They will learn the best gift to give one another is love, unconditional Christ-like love.

How are you giving today? What does the act of giving mean to you?

God, please show me all the ways to give so that I am not limited in my giving. I know You want me to give abundantly, as You give. Thank you, Jesus for giving me a heart that desires to give and bless others. Amen.

Lifted Reflections...

_____

_____

_____

_____

_____

_____

_____

_____

_____

_____

_____

_____

_____

_____

_____

_____

_____

_____

Listen to your Heart

"Each person should do as he has decided in his heart — not reluctantly or out of compulsion, since God loves a cheerful giver. And God is able to make every grace overflow to you, so that in every way, always having everything you need, you may excel in every good work." - 2 Corinthians 9:7-8

"Obey God and listen to your heart," I say to myself often. There were many years in my life that I didn't understand the connection between my heart and God. There are times I am still unclear, but the clarity always comes when I am in the Word and pray. When I seek God, He answers and guides my actions. It is my job to listen, act and obey. Thank you Jesus for showing me the way. I am a cheerful giver when I seek your ways above my own.

What is your heart telling you to do?

God, I am finding the balance to do what is on my heart, not reluctantly or out of compulsion, but with a cheerful spirit. I ask that You continue to guide me to follow my heart for less of me and more of You. I want my giving to be motivated by You and not by my fleshly desires. In Jesus' Name, Amen.

Lifted Reflections...

Live a full life

"The thief comes only to steal and kill and destroy; I have come that they may have life, and have it to the full." - John 10:10

I will guard my heart and live life to the full. I will break patterns that allow me to live in fear or question my worth. He bought me with a high price. Only when I live loved and allow myself to receive the love that He provides, will my own children know and believe in their worth as well. It's time to break this cycle and live in the peace, joy and the abundance of His presence.

Are there any changes you need to make to live a more abundant and prosperous life?

God, You have come so that we may have life and have it to the full. Please reveal to us the ways that we can live a more abundant and prosperous life in Your name. Amen.

Lifted Reflections...

_____

_____

_____

_____

_____

_____

_____

_____

_____

_____

_____

_____

_____

_____

_____

_____

_____

New Beginnings

"Commit to the Lord whatever you do, and he will establish your plans." - Proverbs 16:3

Change is coming, but what kind of change is coming? I commit to do what He guides me to do. I commit my ways to the Lord. I will trust in Him and lean not on my own understanding. I will choose faith over fear and faith over feelings...over and over again. His ways are higher than my own. This I believe and this I will do.

What kind of change does your heart desire? Are you ready for a new beginning in this area of your life?

God, I think I'm ready for new beginnings, but I know I'm in a season of preparation. I will wait expectantly and patiently until Your perfect timing reveals itself. In Jesus' Name, Amen.

Lifted Reflections...

_____

_____

_____

_____

_____

_____

_____

_____

_____

_____

_____

_____

_____

_____

_____

_____

Trust your place in life right now

"For we live by faith, not by sight." - 2 Corinthians 5:7

Trust your place in this life right now. God is preparing you during this season, in this very moment. There is a purpose deeper than you realize. Have faith in Him and seek His guidance today. He will reveal the next step at exactly the right time, for we walk by faith and not by sight.

Lord, I know that there is power for living today as I submit my life to You. Thank You for the grace that empowers me to walk in obedience. Amen.

How are you trusting your place in life right now? Are you currently in a valley, climbing a mountain or standing on the mountaintop? Are you in the middle of a storm? Just coming out of a storm? Or are you preparing for the next storm?

God, I trust my place in life right now. I may not like all of what it entails, but I do see the blessings and I'm thankful that no matter where I am or where I'm going that You are with me every step of the way and You have already prepared the beautiful path that lies ahead. In Jesus' Name, Amen.

Lifted Reflections...

Less me more Him

When Jesus spoke again to the people, he said, "I am the light of the world. Whoever follows me will never walk in darkness, but will have the light of life." - John 8:12

It is so easy to get distracted by the pull of the darkness in our world. We must battle the darkness with His light. This is definitely a season of darkness in more ways than one. I will be sure to get in the Word and put on the full armor of God so that I am prepared to battle the darkness with His love and light.

How is God calling you to live less for you and more for Him?

God, I choose to follow You and walk as light in this dark world. In Jesus' Name, Amen.

Lifted Reflections...

Wake up and be alert

"Be alert and of sober mind. Your enemy the devil prowls around like a roaring lion looking for someone to devour." - 1 Peter 5:8

I woke up at 3:00 AM to my mind saying "1 Peter 5:8" over and over again. In my grogginess I ignored it and tried to fall back asleep, but after about the third time of this and only this repeating in my head.."1 Peter 5:8"...I turned my bedside lamp on and looked it up. This is the only time in my life I've woken up with a verse on my mind like this. This is the scripture that woke me up in the middle of the night. Wow! I hear you God. I'm listening. I'm alert!

When was the last time you had a restless night? Do you think God may be trying to get some intimate alone time with you?

God, You amaze me. Thank you for waking me up so that I live my life according to Your will. May I always turn to You for direction and guidance. You are a good, good Father. Amen.

Lifted Reflections...

Obey God

"He was guilty of no sin, neither was deceit (guile) ever found on His lips. When He was reviled and insulted, He did not revile or offer insult in return; [when] He was abused and suffered, He made no threats [of vengeance]; but He trusted [Himself and everything] to Him Who judges fairly." - 1 Peter 2: 22–23

When we are obedient to God and what He has called us to do, it doesn't always make sense. His ways are higher than our own. We do not lean on our own understanding. Continue to put on love and walk in obedience, regardless of how you feel. Show up and do His work. Pay no mind to the attacks of the enemy. God's got your back! He will take care of things in His time and in His way. Rise above and choose love!

When is it hard to obey God?

God, I have a hard time obeying You when it comes to the things that I want to do for my own flesh. Help me to live less for myself and more for You. Help me to understand that by obeying You I will receive the very best from You. I don't want anything in this life that is not from You. In Jesus' Name, I pray. Amen.

Lifted Reflections...

_____

_____

_____

_____

_____

_____

_____

_____

_____

_____

_____

_____

_____

_____

_____

_____

Let light shine through darkness

"For God, who said, "Let light shine out of darkness," made his light shine in our hearts to give us the light of the knowledge of God's glory displayed in the face of Christ." - 2 Corinthians 4:6

I'm so thankful for the people in this world that get out and represent the heart of Christ. The people who act with love and kindness, that are striving to add value to the lives of others, those are the people that truly make our world a better place. When it is all said and done, those that walk in love are the ones that make a lasting difference in this, often times, dark world.

Who do you know that shines light in darkness, who consistently represents the heart of Christ?

God, I am so thankful to know people who represent Your heart. Their faith encourages mine and I'm grateful to be surrounded by Your army of true Christians who consistently shine Your light through the darkness. Amen.

Lifted Reflections...

_____

_____

_____

_____

_____

_____

_____

_____

_____

_____

_____

_____

_____

_____

_____

_____

_____

Go in Peace

"Your faith has saved you; go in peace." - Luke 7:50

Jesus is constantly offering us His perfect peace. Choose to walk in faith so you can receive and feel the kind of peace only He can give. When we face trials, we are being prepared for the next level. Be thankful and open to receiving His peace in order to be lifted by His presence.

How has your faith saved you? Or how are you hoping your faith will save you?

God, only You can satisfy the burning desire in my heart. Increase my faith to trust in You to bring the desires of my heart to pass. You are the author and finisher of my faith. In Jesus' Name, I pray. Amen.

Lifted Reflections…

_____

_____

_____

_____

_____

_____

_____

_____

_____

_____

_____

_____

_____

_____

_____

_____

_____

Serve & reflect His image

"He must become greater; I must become less." - John 3:30

I tend to want to control the outcome of things happening in my life and in the lives of those I love. I am learning to release the need to control the outcome as I grow in faith. Less of me and more of Him. I would rather live my live to serve and reflect His image, than I would my own. He must become greater and I must become less. I humbly choose to live my life to serve and honor Him.

How does God want you to get out into the world and reflect His image?

God, give me a clear sense of my calling so I can be the best I can possibly be in Your name. I simply want to serve and be a reflection of You. In Jesus' Name, Amen.

Lifted Reflections...

_____

_____

_____

_____

_____

_____

_____

_____

_____

_____

_____

_____

_____

_____

_____

_____

_____

Give it to God & Grow

"Return to your rest, my soul, for the Lord has been good to you." - Psalm 116:7

Give it to God and rest. He will make a way. His ways are higher than our own. Stay in faith no matter how hard the enemy tries to tempt you with lies and fear-based thoughts. Rebuke the lies and persevere in steadfast faith through unceasing prayer and unwavering belief.

What do you do to give it to God? How do you give it to Him and leave it with Him?

God, there are times that I truly want to give it to You and let it go. Please teach me to give it to You completely and not try to pick it up again. You have been good to me and I trust You. I will do my best to give it to You so I can grow in my faith for You to do only what You can do. In Jesus' Name, Amen.

Lifted Reflections...

_____

_____

_____

_____

_____

_____

_____

_____

_____

_____

_____

_____

_____

_____

_____

_____

Suddenly She Knew

"Now may the God of hope fill you with all joy and peace in believing, so that you may overflow with hope by the power of the Holy Spirit." - Romans 15:13

And suddenly she knew...she was the daughter of the King, and her heart will never be the same. Living lifted in His presence is the greatest gift of all.

What do you suddenly know? Are you ready to live lifted?

God, I ask that You begin a good work in the hearts and minds of the people who are reading this devotional. May they be blessed and live lifted in Your presence. In Jesus' Name, Amen.

Lifted Reflections...

_____

_____

_____

_____

_____

_____

_____

_____

_____

_____

_____

_____

_____

_____

_____

_____

_____

Mary Teresa's Commitment through Christ

I will give my personal best.
I will be the positive change I wish to see.
I will listen with my eyes, ears and heart.
I will smile. I will support. I will serve.
I will look for the good in myself and others.
I will spend my time on solutions.
I will be intentional about living with purpose and passion.
I will be a courageous, kind and thoughtful woman who serves
as an example of excellence.
I will strive to bring out the best in others by living with truth,
compassion, grace, integrity and understanding.
I will add value to the lives of others.
I will make a meaningful difference.
I will do all things through Christ who strengthens me.
In Jesus' Name, Amen.

Acknowledgements

I thank my parents, my family and all the people who have been a part of my life. God has placed each person on my path to grow me in Him.

I am beyond grateful for the loving family and friends who have lifted me up during times I needed to experience the love of God through others.

I am grateful for the painful experiences that have brought me closer to Him.

I thank God for giving me new life and leading me to write this devotional to honor and glorify His name.

I thank YOU, the person reading this, for YOU are the reason that God placed it on my heart to publish this devotional. You are loved and He wants your heart. I pray that YOU receive what you need to be lifted by his love. In Jesus' Name, Amen.

What is Your Commitment to & through Christ?

_____

_____

_____

_____

_____

_____

_____

_____

_____

_____

_____

_____

_____

_____

_____

_____

What are your goals?

_____

_____

_____

_____

_____

_____

_____

_____

_____

_____

_____

_____

_____

_____

_____

_____

_____

What do you need to do to be "Lifted" higher?

_____

_____

_____

_____

_____

_____

_____

_____

_____

_____

_____

_____

_____

_____

_____

_____

_____

Made in the USA
Coppell, TX
21 January 2021

48596651R00136